Travel Mementos

Julie Watson taught in countries around the world and in UK higher education before retiring to the Isle of Wight in 2016. She has published research in her academic field and has travelled extensively during her career. Soon after coming to live on the island, she took up kayaking, joined the Wight Writers group and started writing up her travel memoirs.

Her first book, Travel Mementos, is a collection of personal stories about some of the faraway places she has visited. She is now writing a second book on an entirely different topic.

When not writing, she teaches English to refugees, paddles her kayak up and down the creeks of the Western Yar and takes an interest in natural history. When at home, she is at the beck and call of a small feline house guest.

Travel Mementos

Personal Stories
about Faraway Places

Julie Watson

BEACHY BOOKS

First published by
Beachy Books Partner Publishing in 2021
(an imprint of Beachy Books Limited)
www.beachybooks.com

1

A CIP catalogue record for this book is available from the
British Library.

ISBN: 9781913894047

Set in Adobe Caslon Pro

This book is dedicated to my parents,
who wondered if I would ever stop travelling.

Contents

Orbis terrarum liber est, et illi qui non commeant modo unam paginam legunt

(author unknown)

Introduction

When I was very young I had a picture book about people from different countries around the world. It was full of stereotypes but I was fascinated by the exotic illustrations of people in national costume holding their country's national dish. There was a map, showing where they all lived. I would study the pictures wondering how and why their lives could be so different from my own. I remember badly wanting to see those places for myself, so much so that a few years later I started writing my own travel stories. These were imaginary rather than actual experiences as I did not find the means to travel until I was older. But those first fictitious attempts were for my own gratification.

One summer, many years later, found me teaching English in a language school in Cambridge. I must have been in my early twenties by then. It was morning coffee break and all the teachers were gathered in the tiny staffroom. Among them was Jacky, an actress if I remember, but she was, as they say, 'resting' between roles. So that summer she was teaching to pay the bills. Somehow the conversation turned to palm reading. Casually, she announced, 'I can read palms. My mother was taught by an Indian Fakir and she taught me.'

'Read mine; read mine!' we all shouted at once, thrusting out our hands but then the bell rang for lessons again. Not to be denied, someone had an idea. By the end of the day we had all visited the photocopier, sandwiched a hand between the glass screen and the lid and pressed the copy button. That evening Jacky took home a stack of anonymous hand copies to read and annotate as well as the usual pile of students' homework to mark.

The next day I reclaimed my photocopy and pored over her reading of the various lines and creases of my palm. I was curious rather than believing. Nevertheless, I still have that piece of paper four decades later. 'This person will travel a lot…,' she had written. This pleased me but then I read, '…and was probably born abroad.' I fulfilled the first prophecy but to my knowledge, not the second—at least, my parents have always told me that I was born in Coventry. Jacky had also written, 'this person could write' (this was underscored I remember) along with 'but lacks willpower.' The latter also turned out to be true. I made a few tentative starts at writing through the years and even had a few articles published but failed to find the necessary commitment to take writing more seriously until I retired. I then had no more excuses.

So I've made it happen. Here are my travel stories. The book contains twenty true stories spanning different continents and cultures. I hope that each conveys a sense of place, time and personal encounter and that you enjoy reading them—in whatever order you choose. The titles are listed below in case you have a favourite geographical region where you would like to start. Lastly, just in case she's on another 'rest' from acting and reading this, my thanks must go to Jacky, woman of many talents, for her prophetic reading of my palm all those years ago!

Rights of Passage (southern Spain)

Table Manners for Eating Noodles (Japan)

Gelato - As It Once Was (Milan, Italy)

The Dance of the Scorpions (Durango, Mexico)

Irish Black Gold (Ireland)

Travels in the Company of P38 (Israel and Egypt)

Displaced on the Spanish Plain (Avila, Spain)

Where Europe Ends (northern Norway)

Blushing Onions and Therapy by the Sea
(Brittany, France)

Lovestruck in Leningrad (Russia)

Seeing Red in the Canary Islands
(Gran Canaria, Spain)

A Hitchhiker's Guide to the Bay of Biscay
(Atlantic Ocean, west of France and north of Spain)

A Ride into the Shadow Underworld
(Jogjakarta, Indonesia)

The Mystery of a Nudge in the Night
(Arctic Circle, Norway)

Birdsong (Rome, Italy)

The Village of Cloves (Sulawesi, Indonesia)

The Misadventure of a Goose
(Norfolk, United Kingdom)

The Last Wood Turner (Toledo, Spain)

A Long Shot (Java, Indonesia)

Senior Moments in Segovia (Spain)

Rights of Passage

We hear the patrol boat before we see it. A motoric throb resonates from deep within the sea mist. White swirls wrap the dark-pitted peaks of Morocco as they float upwards, mysterious and intangible in the distance.

Their presence reaches out to us, fourteen kilometres away, where we sit on a Spanish beach, scanning the sky with binoculars for specks—specks that could turn out to be honey buzzards, rare black storks or multi-coloured bee-eaters—any bird of passage with wings of courage to make the short dash over the stomach-churning straits between Europe and Africa in search of a warmer winter on another continent.

Atlantic meets Mediterranean here: one grey-wild and frothy, the other blue and volatile. But high above the clashing seas, no birds are making the crossing today. The giant fin whales also eluded us on our boat trip yesterday. No spurting blows or surface-lying logs eyeing us curiously. Those juggernauts of the sea had passed silently through the deep trench beneath us.

Only the high-spirited dolphins tumbled around our dancing boat, their airborne bodies curling in delight as queasy passengers on the deck leaned seawards to part with their breakfast. We were hoping to see more than this.

Instead, this afternoon we hear the patrol boat, see its sleek black body emerge briefly in a mist-free window before it speeds off towards the African coast. Then more sound—the slapping of helicopter blades as one dips down out of the sky onto Las Palomas—the Isle of Doves. Barely an island, this rocky outcrop marks the southernmost point of continental Europe.

Yesterday evening we walked the kilometre-long causeway linking it to Tarifa on the mainland, halting at its padlocked gate. Frustrated, we stood and peered through the bars. Around us on the sea, exuberant kite surfers swooped and raced, the Levante wind whipping them into the air and across the waves in wild ecstatic joy.

Las Palomas was once a military fort, the guidebook said. In recent times, a detention centre for 'illegals'—mostly young African men, washed ashore in collapsed rubber dinghies. Full of hope, they have spilled out onto the sands of a New World.

An air of secrecy hangs over the fort now. A concealed compound lies at its centre—there, we can just make out some low abandoned barrack buildings, visible only with binoculars from the beach. But perhaps they are not altogether abandoned. Earlier, an unmarked white delivery van crossed the causeway and was admitted through the gates. It left soon afterwards, the closing metal clanking heavily behind it.

Now we turn our binoculars on the helicopter; noting its stiff tail and bulbous cockpit eye. Inside, its belly is crammed with shadowy human outlines. Impossible to say how many.

It descends onto the island disappearing into the dark heart, blade noise muffled into silence.

We sit, watching, waiting, and squeeze the soft white sand between our toes. The waves, dark with seaweed, quietly lap and curl gently towards us.

Suddenly, the sound of the helicopter reverberates across the water once again. Lighter now with its cargo discharged, it rises like an aggravated insect, before disappearing back into the mist.

We put away our binoculars and look back at the sea, troubled, but knowing we can breathe the salty air of freedom enjoyed by migrating birds and boat-shy whales as they journey through their borderless world.

Table Manners for Eating Noodles

Summoning up my courage, I walked into the ramen-ya. I was a newly arrived foreigner, a gaijin, in a brightly lit noodle shop in a small Japanese town, and I wouldn't go unnoticed. But I was hungry and wanted to try the house speciality.

On the menu board outside, the large knot of brown noodles floating in a soupy sea looked appetising enough. I had read that ramen had been eaten since ancient Edo times and were so popular they could claim to be Japan's national dish. I was keen to try them.

After studying the picture carefully, I tentatively placed my order, persuaded by the slivers of pork and nori seaweed in amongst the noodles, Cubes of white tofu and chopped scallions floated on the surface.

I sat down at a table and waited for my order. Feeling nervous, I glanced quickly around the restaurant. The only other customers were a Japanese family of four, too busy eating to pay the gaijin much attention. I relaxed.

In front of me lay a small paper envelope from which a pair of waribashi protruded—throwaway bamboo chopsticks, split halfway and ready for use. I knew about them from my book on

Japanese etiquette. I fingered them lightly, resisting the desire to pull them apart immediately.

The waiter arrived with my noodles. 'Douzo,' he said, and with a slight bow he placed a steaming bowl before me. I waited for him to leave then snapped the chopsticks apart. A clean break—good. I dipped them into the noodle knot, exploring, and taking care not to spear.

Concentrating like a surgeon, I teased a loose noodle strand from the slippery mass. I clasped it firmly and raised it to my mouth, remembering to suck gently without slurping too much. So far so good.

Hearing a sound, my chopsticks trembled in my hand. I froze momentarily over my noodle bowl and raised my head. On the neighbouring table, four pairs of eyes were closely watching my movements. With my confidence evaporating, I looked down at the noodles again and considered what I might have done wrong. Too much slurping perhaps, or not enough?

I had remembered to raise the bowl, my chopsticks were correctly positioned. The upper one held like a pencil one third of the way down, the other set against it balanced between finger and thumb. Inexpert though I was, I hadn't lost control of them or let a noodle escape. What then?

'Hidari-kiki?' she asked. Smiling shyly, the mother nodded towards my still suspended left hand. Hidari-kiki? Left-handed? Then it dawned on me. I was eating with my left hand, in a country where less than ten percent of the population were lefties.

Here the norm was right-handedness. Everything was designed to serve the right-handed population. From ancient

Japanese art of calligraphy to modern convenience. Whether executing a brush stroke in ink or operating a hot drink vending machine, you needed to use your right hand. So while my perfect table manners had gone unnoticed, my left-handedness certainly hadn't.

Gelato - As It Once Was

'Scusi c'è una gelateria qui vicino?' I enquire at the hotel front desk. It's the last evening of my return visit to Milan and I still haven't enjoyed the pleasure of Italian ice cream. With a knowing smile, the receptionist points in the direction of the nearby square. 'Si Signora, nella piazza a destra. Si chiama Grom.'

It's called Grom? I must look sceptical but I suspend my disbelief and thank him. Privately, I doubt that a gelateria sounding like a road haulage company will serve good ice cream.

Stepping out of the air-conditioned lobby is like immersing myself in a warm bath. Siesta time is over; the city is coming back to life. And the shops have re-opened. Sylphlike young women are already strolling out, talking animatedly on their mobile phones, Armani and Gucci carrier bags swinging from slim wrists and carefully manicured hands. Fashion shopping isn't on my itinerary any longer—my own 'sylphlike' figure abandoned me a while ago—but it's nice to see that it's still taken seriously here in Milan.

I turn right at the corner, a destra as instructed, and need to skirt the edge of a sea of outdoor café tables spilling in all directions across the pavement. Most are occupied by youthful

Milanese, wholesome and healthy-looking, sitting with one of their five a day in front of them. No water bottles are in sight. Is drinking fruit juice a new trend, I wonder? Peach, orange, pineapple and pear are casually scattered across the table tops, their colours reproduce the happy mood of a Miró composition, but I notice a Peroni beer and the illusion is broken.

That essential fashion accessory for any self-respecting millennial, the mobile phone, is everywhere. Lying in readiness or held in use. One, in the hand of a young man who has stepped out of a Caravaggio painting, starts to tinkle its theme tune. A tee-shirt sculpts another's well-toned torso and my eyes are momentarily held. 'Ciao Bello,' I murmur to myself, while enjoying the fleeting image of taking an aperitivo with a toyboy.

I move on and a waft of warm air stirs the café awning as I pass under it. Since I arrived I've been wondering if I will find Milan changed. It's been twenty years since my last trip here. A part of the older and more worldly-wise me is prepared for disappointment. I remember some cautionary advice about return visits: if you go to a place twice, each time it's a different story. But the world is a finite place and revisiting a haunt of the past seems to happen to me more often as the years go by.

I reach the square and there is Gelateria Grom, proudly displaying its claim to offer 'il gelato come una volta'. Ice cream as it once was. The promise fills me with hope but I'm surprised to find a line of people standing outside the small ice cream kiosk. A queue? Since when has queuing been part of Italian culture? Secretly, I'm reassured. Ice cream that you need to wait for must be worth it.

I survey the scene: a gaggle of laughing school friends, an oblivious couple enjoying a romantic moment; parents with bambini in state-of-the-art buggies. It's a cross-section of Milanese society, all hungry for gelato. I add myself behind the last in the line and study the ice cream board.

The list is impressively long and a masterpiece of inventiveness. My eyes flit between the 'classici' and 'speciali', trying to take them all in. Some of the specialities induce thrills of mouth-tingling anticipation—chestnut, ricotta and fig, cassata, one with extract of liquorice and the wildly exotic flavour of the month—cream of saffron. Am I feeling bold enough to experiment today?

The quickened tempo of rising voices in the queue ahead distracts me from my decision-making. A passionate argument breaks out. Someone is trying to push in and has been noticed. Orderly line formation is proving to be a challenging concept.

Despite the general air of conviviality, everyone has been keeping a sharp eye out for wily queue-jumpers. These are street-wise Italians, after all. My ears start to attune to the rising voices and that familiar underlying melodious sound as they engage in lively exchanges of opinion again. It takes me back and is strangely comforting. After a moment the eruption subsides, pitches descend and voices settle back into a steady conversational rhythm. The ice cream queue radiates confident expectation once more.

Little by little, our unruly line is being swallowed into the mouth of the kiosk. We ripple forward like a caterpillar, each segment holding its place. From the exit people are appearing, loaded with full tubs and towering cones. My turn is fast approaching. Hopefully, Grom will not disappoint.

The woman in front has placed a large order. I am grateful and use the opportunity to review the list for one last time. Then I'm at the counter, squashed up against the glass and feeling like a pressed flower.

'Prego Signora?' Help! I hesitate for a fatal moment, and miss out on the flavour of the month experience, instead ordering a safe double classic—pistacchio and cioccolato, and just 'un cono piccolo, per favore.' Fear has held me back.

Then with Olympic gelato held high, I emerge, feeling mildly victorious. Outside, there is a small space on a nearby bench, between a mobile owner and a fellow cone carrier. I squeeze myself into it.

My ice cream is already protesting about the heat and escaping in drips. Time to act. I raise the cone. My tongue reaches out. I close my eyes and smile—gelato as it once was—there are some things, thankfully, which haven't changed.

The Dance of the Scorpions

'Alacran!' White teeth light up the face of the Mexican stallholder as he grins and gestures towards his scorpion wares. There, dangling among colourful ceramic pots and ponchos, are bundles of keyrings. A scorpion is attached to each, interred in a plastic chamber and suspended in the sleep of death.

My gaze wanders, taking in ashtrays, clocks and other scorpion-embellished bric-a-brac: everywhere I see Centruriodes suffusus, the unwilling star of the local souvenir industry. Feigning a smile, I move on. I'm pinning my hopes on seeing a live specimen.

I have read about this scorpion, a native of the dry northern deserts around the city of Durango but also a migrant here, living secretly side by side with the human residents. It keeps a low profile but has a tough life. Hiding skills don't help much in the face of an army of alacraneros (scorpion hunters) whose own livelihoods depend on collecting it each day.

I leave behind the vibrant colours and sweet vegetable smells of the indoor market and am swallowed up in the anarchy of the street. The heat and dust hit me. Dodging the traffic, I slip into the cool interior of the university building; a faded three-storey affair in Spanish colonial style, and where I am temporarily sharing an office during my stay.

Up to the second floor in the lift. A bouncy, jarring ride. There is a buzz of excitement as I enter. Surprised, I glance around. And then a collegial hand offers me a glass container. I take a step backwards; inside are two scorpions, captive and agitated.

Somewhere deep within the dry adobe walls of the building, a wrong turn was taken. A mistake that brought these scorpions into dangerous human terrain. My Mexican friends have detained them in the office for my benefit.

I take a closer look and see two yellow-brown bodies, flattened like Formula One racing cars. Each is armed with a pair of needle-thin pincers that give a menacing wave to distract attention from their business end—a tail loaded with a potent pouch of venom that can effortlessly kill a healthy adult.

'Le gustaría verlos? Ven conmigo por favor,' Jose Miguel, a technician and the self-appointed scorpion handler, leads me up to the flat roof and there we gingerly open the jar. Scorpions tumble onto concrete. Liberated but with no place to hide, they are uncertain in these new surroundings. Then, recovering, they begin to move about jerkily as if to an inaudible music. Two silent flamenco dancers: pincers held high, executing short coordinated steps. Their dance is intense and indignant.

Under the hot Latin American sun, I watch them perform, mesmerised by synchronised footwork, beckoning pincers and beguiling curved tails. Abruptly, I feel a wave of remorse. I did not wish this venue or these circumstances on them, and I fear what the future holds for this species.

'Gracias,' I mumble. My scorpion-handler, circles at a respectful distance, gently coaxing them back into the jar with a long stick. Later I learn that an evolutionary quirk is helping in their fight for survival. Interbreeding with a species from nearby Zacatecas, the Durango scorpion has transformed itself into an even more deadly hybrid. There is hope.

Rooftop performance over, I accompany Jose Miguel to release my flamenco stars in the desert far from human territory. There, they will live to dance another day.

Irish Black Gold

From the window of the farmhouse nestled deep inside Ireland's Iveragh Peninsula, I can make out a distant black strip of land. Puzzled, I turn to Mary, my homestay host, and ask if something is growing out there. Mary glances to where I am pointing. 'Oh God, no! Nothin,' she replies in a rich Irish brogue, 'It's the peat bog.'

I notice the basket in the corner and the lumpy black clods it contains, sprouting hair-like bits of stick and straw and with a faint smell reminiscent of fresh earth. I realise it's peat, dug out from the nearby fen.

I have been making my way slowly around the twists and turns of the Wild Atlantic Way. This meandering route that skirts the west coast of Ireland and offers tantalising glimpses of long sandy beaches as it winds its way around craggy peninsulas jutting out into the swelling ocean. And each day I ask myself again why it has taken me so long to discover the stunning scenery and diverse wildlife here.

The flocks of face-painted puffins nesting in the cliffs have entranced me, awkward and waddling on the rocks but transformed into small fat torpedoes in the water. Bouncy pods of dolphins were churning up the sea spray around our boat as we circumnavigated the Blasket islands, Europe's most westerly point. I have stared eyeball to eyeball with spy-hopping grey seals as we chugged past. Another day, a hike across the creviced limestone slabs of fossilised coral and grassy fields that form the Burren landscape, inhabited since Neolithic times and bursting with wild orchids and other calcium loving plants in late spring. Otters and orcas followed. I feel as if I have stepped straight into a BBC Natural History filmset.

Mary's voice brings me back to the matter of peat. 'It's the best thing for starting a fire,' she continues. A fire is something I can hardly imagine today. Ireland is parching under a long heatwave—the hottest and driest June since 1976. Out here on the Atlantic facing side of the country, cold wet weather is supposedly the norm, and for months on end. For such times, Mary has a peat supply on her doorstep, delivered by her neighbour at 300 euros a tractor load. This slow-burning, almost smokeless fuel lasts her five months before she needs to replenish her stock.

Over the next few days, I begin to recognise the dark tell-tale sign of peat extraction on the landscape all around me. I'm struck by the abundance of this earthy black gold everywhere. Such an important part of Irish heritage. These peat bogs are said to stretch over one sixth of the country and are thousands of years in the making. But today the minds of the local peat farmers on the peninsula are firmly on the work in hand. Like their fathers and grandfathers before them, they are busy at their livelihood—making peat briquettes while the sun shines. Wielding slanes, their traditional cutting tools, they are slicing out rectangular sods of soft fresh peat.

I stop to watch for a while as an old farmer toils under the fierce sun. Nearby, a flashing metallic dragonfly patrols the pools of black water rising up to fill the ditches left behind.

Neat lines of freshly cut black bars are rapidly baking hard while others stand propped together into miniature crooked wigwams. In this year's exceptionally good conditions, the drying process is taking just two weeks. Tractors laden with peat bullion are moving unhurriedly along the roads, tailed by lines of thwarted traffic.

It is a bucolic picture. Mary was wrong. The peat bog *is* something. A heritage to be proud of—but for how much longer will it be there? I turn away from the scene and look again at the black pools. The dragonfly has gone.

Travels in the Company of P38

Lockdown time produces some strange compulsions! Rummaging through a kitchen drawer I have unearthed a small metal tool. As I hold it between my fingers, an old memory sheds its cloak of cobwebs and resurfaces for inspection.

The object is nearly forty years old now and showing signs of corrosion from much use. It has a personal history, which I will shortly explain. It's flat, rectangular and about three centimetres in length. A small round eyelet has been punched out of one end so that it can be attached to a piece of string or a keyring. This was a useful afterthought of the designer, as it is a small item that could easily be lost. It has an edge shaped into a wavelike curve ending in a pointed lip. Another side is bent into the form of a triangular cutter, which can be quite lethal if you inadvertently get your finger in the way while operating it. I know this to my cost. There is some writing engraved on it—three lines of Hebrew characters. I don't know what they mean but they probably say something like multi-purpose opener. For that is what the object is, and it has served me to open many a soft drink bottle, can of tuna or jar of preserves while travelling. For some reason, it is known as a P38[1].

It came into my possession in 1984 and after that we became inseparable travelling companions. I was taking some time out, what would nowadays be called a 'gap year', and was working for my keep, rotating between the communal laundry and kitchen, the cotton field and the plastics factory of a kibbutz on the coast of Israel. Appropriately called Nahsholim or The Waves, I had selected it by stabbing a finger on a map in the Kibbutz Volunteering Office a few days after my arrival in Tel Aviv. Nahsholim sat on the silky sands of the Mediterranean, like a child playing in the warm shallow waters of a long curving stretch of azure sea, protected inland by the maternal gaze of Mount Carmel.

After scrubbing tomatoes free of herbicide in the kibbutz kitchen or endlessly ironing shirts in the laundry I would take a long idyllic walk along the beach, stopping occasionally to examine some curious nobbly orange lumps that protruded from the white sand. I puzzled over them for a long time before realising that they were the sea-tumbled fragments of terracotta amphorae, worn smooth by the waves of centuries and cast up on the shore. Each was once a joint piece, the place where a handle met an elegant neck or the curvaceous body of a Greco-Roman urn. The thumb prints where the Roman potter

---

1   *While writing this I researched my P38 to find out how it got its name. It seems that it was originally developed in the 1940s in the USA and supplied to soldiers with their field rations. The story goes that it could open a can faster than its namesake, the P-38 Lightning fighter plane, could fly.*

had pressed them on were still visible. After a lifetime spent transporting olives, wine or oil between the ancient Mediterranean ports, they lay broken and dormant in one of the many wrecks lying on the seabed just offshore, before washing up to their final resting place on the beach of Nahsholim.

Sometimes my afternoon walks and archaeological musings were shattered by the deafening noise overhead of an Israeli jet ripping a hole in the sky as it flew north towards Lebanon on a practice exercise or maybe a military mission. I never knew which, and back then, my untroubled younger self chose not to dwell on this. I also preferred not to reflect too much on the role of the plastic military parts produced by the injection moulding machines that we volunteers operated in the factory. But I should return to the story of my P38.

Towards the end of my stay in Israel, wanderlust gripped me again and I bought a return bus ticket to Egypt. Asking in the kibbutz kitchen for some provisions for the journey, I was given some tins of tuna fish and a stack of pitta bread. I considered the tins for a moment during which the cook must have read my mind. She handed me a P38 and so began our first trip together.

The long meandering coastal road took us westwards past flat and fertile plains of citrus fruit and avocado. Then our bus swept into the Gaza strip, claustrophobically cramped and poverty-stricken but unenclosed in those days. Out again and into the Sinai Peninsula, passing between the sweeping expanse of desert on one side and the intense blue seascape on the other.

Every few hours we made a rest stop and I would take out some pitta bread, and apply my handy little opener to a can of tuna.

Eventually a thin ribbon of light appeared far ahead of us lying across the road and glittering in the sun. The silhouette of a ship moved silently down it and into the desert. A mirage? For a moment I was disoriented by this strange apparition. Then we were crossing it—the Suez Canal. To celebrate, I tore off more pitta bread and reached for my P38 and another tin of tuna. Onwards to Cairo.

In the weeks that followed together we travelled 600 or so kilometres down the Nile, taking in all the must-see places of Egypt, first the pyramids at Giza and then the temples of Karnak and Luxor. At Luxor I crossed the river and, hiring a bicycle, in a moment of madness, I rode out in the noonday sun to the Valley of the Kings. Next stop was the Temple of Isis, a further 200 kilometres downstream. A boat took us out to the island where it now stands, after being dismantled and moved to escape submersion during the building of the Aswan Dam. At this point, the road south ended for us. Inland the desert beckoned so we turned towards it and hopped from one oasis settlement to another with the help of a succession of lifts from local truck drivers all the way back to Cairo. I recall the long desert drive with one of them in particular. He had a Demis Roussos cassette tape from the 1970s, which he played continuously as we bounced our way across the sand. Even today, many years later, I cannot think of desert landscapes without the strains of Roussos's love song, *Forever and Ever*, flooding my ears.

Along our circuitous route I restocked with more canned tuna from small Egyptian stores and my trusty metal companion dangled from its string on my backpack, always at the ready to slit and disembowel their contents or to flip off the caps from bottles of the local Sprite. This was usually warm and flat but became my choice of thirst quencher in the hot afternoon sun. Eventually my Egyptian adventure and 'time out' in Israel came to an end. Reluctantly, I returned home to look for work, with P38 still optimistically swinging from my pack, perhaps in anticipation of our next trip together.

Now, so many years later, as I turn it over in my hand and notice those Hebrew characters again, I hesitate. To throw it into the charity bag or keep it? I take a tea towel and attempt to restore its shine, then replace it gently in the kitchen drawer. After all, its travelling days, like mine, are not necessarily over yet.

Displaced on the Spanish Plain

This morning I am leaving the hotel with a headful of television images. Over breakfast I learned that Catalonia is declaring independence from Spain. The plazas are crowded in Barcelona and Madrid; with scenes resembling surging whirlpools. Protesters for independence or for national unity. Randomly, eruptions of mayhem flash across the screen.

Convoluted legal debates were taking place in the television studio. But the arguments confused me, an outsider, travelling in an unfamiliar land. Outside the hotel I pause and re-orientate myself, then set off towards the Estación de Tren de Salamanca. Perhaps a day inside the medieval walls of Avila will offer some relief from a troubled present.

We leave precisely on time. The October sky is clear blue. Fields, stubbled with gold, stretch far across the plain, melting invisibly into the distant sierra. High up, a ropey formation of Griffon vultures effortlessly rides a warm thermal, searching for carrion below.

The train from Salamanca is almost empty and carries me eastwards. Avila was the home of Teresa, saint, mystic and, according to my guidebook, a discalced Carmelite nun. Discalced. The fields drift by outside as I crack the word in two like an egg, looking for meaning inside.

I delve back into my guidebook, the 1500s and Teresa of Avila, living here on the Spanish plain. And discalced? I turn a page. Here it is—'without shoes.' Hers was a strict religious order; the nuns went barefoot.

For a while I read on about this woman of visions and ecstatic trances, living out her life of austerity and contemplation in difficult times. Then the gentle rocking of the train lulls me into sleepiness. I lean against the window and let the plain and sky wash over me until the train coasts gently into Avila station.

A straight road leads to the old walled town ending at its imposing eleventh century gateway. Somewhere inside is a convent, built over her birthplace. But first I meet an unexpected maze of cobbled streets. I am not alone here. Other visitors have arrived ahead of me and long pilgrim processions, as well as confusing signposts, bar my way.

I drift around helplessly, lost for a time. When the museum dedicated to her life and work reveals itself, the door is closed. In the nearby gift shop the man at the counter just shrugs, unable or unwilling to explain when it might re-open.

I wander away, and by chance, arrive at another highlight on the Teresa tour, the Monasterio de la Encarnación. Open, and displaying the monastic cell where she lived for forty years. The nun in charge leads me to a wooden door, which she opens with an outsized iron key. She demonstrates the bell pulley for calling to be let out. Then I am alone, feeling slightly disconcerted, and enclosed in a room full of curious personal effects in ageing glass cabinets. I approach one of them.

Parchment scraps, covered in a faded cryptic writing of enigmatic loops and curls, Teresa relics—the ossified ring finger of her right hand, a walking stick, a flagellation rope. My eyes wander restlessly. I notice a small cell in the corner of the room, a stone wall and a hard chair.

I inspect the contents of more cabinets, curious, but feeling like an intruder. Our lives are centuries apart. It's hard to find connections. I take a step towards the bell pulley; then stop. Lying among the relics is a loop of misshapen brown beads. No, they are not real beads but acorns. It must be a prayer rosary: a homemade one. Her own. Local acorns collected after an autumn fall and threaded together. After a lifetime of use they are worn smooth by handling and darkly weathered. I am somehow touched by this. A deeply personal possession, it has survived the turmoil of the centuries and now quietly bides its time here.

Later, on the train back to Salamanca, a scene drifts before my mind's eye. A woman, barefoot, sitting on a hard chair, fingers methodically working dry acorns. She's praying in silence and crossing the threshold into an ineffable elsewhere. Taking a step into eternity.

My vision is broken by the sound of the guard passing through. The passenger opposite me is reading a newspaper; its front page displays turbulent scenes in the Spanish capital. I am thrust back into the uneasy present. Teresa said, 'Life is like a night in a bad hotel.' Her world or mine? Outside, the fields slip by endlessly as the plain unravels, marked only by a solitary oak tree.

Where Europe Ends

A forest of squelchy moss lies under our feet. It's unwilling to let us pass and sucks at our boots as we, the walkers, trudge along. Here and there, the heavy raised heads of sunken boulders watch silently. I fear they are mythical Nordic giants buried deep in the earth. Some are crowned with curly wigs of bleached green lichen; others, tattooed with a patchwork of black lines—the aptly named map lichen. We stop walking and sink deeper into this primeval world. It's still drizzling as we pore over our own map, which is already soggy despite its plastic sleeve. I shake the cold compass back to life. We study the map, confer and make a 60 degree turn to the left. It's that way...we think.

We are in the far north of Norway, midnight sun territory high above the Arctic Circle, and we have been lost for some hours; perhaps stumbling around in circles. The northernmost end of continental Europe is not far from here. But which way? This peninsula is called Knivskjellodden—it's a finger of land pointing prophetically out across the wild North Sea towards the North Pole, 2000 or so kilometres away. Its fingertip is actually one and a half kilometres further north than North Cape, the tourist destination, which we have scornfully turned our backs on. The coastal E69 route ends there, but we have stopped a few kilometres short and parked our car on the road-side. To reach our goal, we have ten more of watery tundra to walk through, and no path.

It's a mystical landscape, bathed in the eerie twilight of a sun that never dips below the horizon at this time of year, and we are not alone here. Without the security of trees, small birds roosting in the boulder crevices flit out, up and away, when disturbed by our footfall. Signs of larger creatures litter the moss around us too. Antlers. The discarded headgear of rein-deer after the rutting season. Some have lain here for months and gleam bone-white in their mossy beds. Others shed more recently, still bear tattered red ribbons of velvet reindeer skin, slowly being eaten away in the rain. Their previous owners are growing new ones now as they wander their summer grazing grounds on the coast.

A curtain of mist has dropped all around. We walk on with tired feet and ebbing confidence. We were supposed to inform the police if we ventured across the tundra, but we didn't. Pre-sumably others, with a thirst for adventure, have also lost their way here. Too late now. We struggle on. Ahead of us the mist stirs, and parts. An apparition moves out of it. Then anoth-er. Shadowy alien shapes slowly materialise into… a herd of reindeer! A straggly line of animals that stops in surprise at the sight of two trespassers in their kingdom. They gaze at us and the silence of the moment is everlasting. A muffled snort breaks the spell, and losing interest, they turn away and resume their foraging.

I try to ignore the dampness that has seeped through my jacket and turned my skin cold. Instead, I concentrate on the ground as I walk, focusing on the tapestry of small plants: red, yellow, brown and green, all clinging to life in this impoverished and saturated soil. More time passes. The small hours have descended but the light persists in this strange, sleepless place. We are walking uphill now—to the sea? This can't be right. But it's just a small ridge, which we pass over. And then! We hear it first. Quite unexpectedly, and music to our ears. The sound of waves tumbling the pebbles on the shore.

We have reached our journey's end. From this ridge above the tideline, we sigh in relief and look out, surveying the foamy water as it breaks on the beach below.

Here at the end of the world, the shore is strewn with flotsam and jetsam. Plant debris has floated in from distant lands, borne on the boisterous waves; other items have been flung off cargo ships in rough seas as they've navigated the shipping lane around the top of Norway. Bits of broken crates with indecipherable markings denoting exotic countries of origin; a jigsaw of unrecognisable twentieth century plastic, water-stressed and reduced to fragments, doomed to last forever. But it is a beachcomber's paradise. We gladly drop our packs, tent and sleeping bags onto the pebbles, flex our weary shoulders and claim our reward, wandering beside the water and gently turning over the shore's treasures with our feet to examine them.

Later, I am standing on an exposed black rock that juts out into the sea, I look towards where the North Pole must surely lie. The wind pummels the hood of my jacket and deep inside, my ears hear these sounds as muffled explosions, drowning out the roar of the ocean. I congratulate myself—from this vantage point I can draw a line between me and the North Pole with nothing in between. We made it to the end of Europe.

Then, something just offshore disturbs the water. The slick and sliding surface parts and a dark mottled head, sleek and whiskery, rises from the depths. The doglike snout of a grey seal: its nostrils open and a pair of alert marble eyes, dark and shiny, regard me curiously as I stare back. My imaginary line has been breached, but now I will always remember this moment. The seal sinks back into the crow-black depths.

It's very late and we are spent. Further up the beach, we unpack and pitch the tent badly, unroll damp sleeping bags and crawl inside for a few hours' sleep. Tomorrow, that is later today, we must find our way back[2].

---

2 *This walk took place in 1997. There is now a marked trail and well-trodden footpath leading across the tundra to the northernmost point of Europe at the end of the Knivskjellodden peninsula.*

Blushing Onions
and Therapy by the Sea

A blast on the foghorn is followed by an apologetic tinkle of music from the ship's intercom, waking its passengers from fitful sleep. The music stops; replaced by polite but firm messages. Their purpose is to eject us from our cabins, ready for disembarkation. I comply, removing myself quickly to escape more intrusion.

Stumbling up the stairs to deck six, I encounter returning French holidaymakers, already milling about with their luggage or in the queue for a quick petit dejeuner. I move through them and step outside to taste the sea tang and inhale some French air. We have arrived.

Protesting like a blunt knife, the Plymouth to Roscoff cross-channel ferry judders as it carves a watery passage into port through rolling morning mist and a swirl of aggrieved seagulls. After a moment, the curtain lifts to reveal a compact line of uneven granite buildings standing like a damp welcome committee on the Brittany shoreline.

We shuffle through passport control and customs, silent and dishevelled, to be cast out into the cold air of the ferry port. With the shadow of sleepiness still dogging me I begin the slow walk up into the small town of Roscoff.

I am not expecting much—perhaps a harbour with a few fishing vessels and a café or two. The prospect feels underwhelming. In any case, I only have a few short hours on French soil before the return leg of the journey.

Gradually, the anonymous port buildings give way to a field of dew-dripping cabbages, announcing arrival in suburbia as we enter the Rue de Plymouth. A line of large detached houses sense us pass by from behind closed hostile shutters.

The mist has drenched everything in its path. In impeccably neat gardens, bedraggled rhododendron bushes sit motionless like plump glistening buddhas, and lanky hollyhocks droop their wet red flowers despondently. I too have been dunked in dampness and begin to wish I hadn't ignored the ship's call to breakfast. How long will I have to wait for a café to open, I wonder. But finally we reach the town's main thoroughfare, and there is one.

Moving figures and the hum of voices draw us in. Ty Pierre. It's already buzzing with locals. What does the name mean? For a fleeting moment I wonder if I have landed in a different country then realise that I am not reading French, but Breton.

I clear my throat and venture the question. The waitress pauses, café au lait in hand, thinks for a moment and then translates it back into French for me. It's simply Chez Pierre, or 'Pierre's Place'.

After ordering a coffee I pick up the local newspaper from the bar. My eyes fall on the lead story and its accompanying picture—a serious Frenchman staring straight at the camera.

He's holding aloft a braid of reddish looking onions. Apparently, a fête de l'oignon has just taken place.

That explains the dozen or so cone-shaped tents we passed, standing forlornly in the Aire de Jeux park near the old port. Around them, a handful of workmen had been slowly dismantling, or stacking empty pallets. But why an onion festival? My interest piqued, I read on.

It seems that the pink onions of Roscoff, are famous. Cultivated locally in a soil and climate which suits them, they generate a lucrative industry. The town chefs transform them into imaginative culinary delicacies, I discover, like lipig—even the sound sticks to my palate as I say it. This thick onion marmalade is the key ingredient of local preserves, soups, caramelised onion tart and other specialities.

Roscoff has been proudly showing off all facets of its celebrity vegetable over the weekend and the festival has attracted traders and growers from all over the region.

There is more. This humble onion has its own historical credentials, which led to an Anglo-French rapprochement. In the 1800s an enterprising Roscovite boarded a boat with his bicycle and crossed the channel in search of a new market for his onions. Dubbed 'Johnnie onion man' by his new Anglo-Saxon customers, his initiative resulted in an armada of peddling 'Johnnies' bringing the taste of France to English shores over the following centuries.

So Roscoff knows about onions. A fishing village with an innovative sideline in a speciality bulb. The onion business diversified and even brings in some extra tourist revenue too, judging from the row of souvenir shops.

The coffee and this discovery perks me up. With a better understanding of Roscoff under my belt, I leave Ty Pierre's to wander along the seafront. The mist has all but disappeared and the tide has ebbed revealing a network of rockpools, lounging the length of the shore and draped in seductive green negligees of seaweedy fronds. These are releasing the unmistakeable scent of sea air. I turn a corner and make another discovery.

To complement its blushing bulbs, Roscoff has cashed in on the abundance of its seaweed resource and established itself as a centre of thalassotherapy. Since 1899, it has been a pioneering resort for sea cures and marine health products deriving from its mineral-rich seaweed and iodized sea air.

Offering body wraps of algae paste, sea fog inhalation and massages, thalassotherapy promises invigorating skin renewal and lung benefits. Becoming the centrepiece of a restorative wrap of seaweed paste sounds like an interesting experience, but my time on shore is almost over. Warmed by the afternoon sun, I walk slowly back down to the ferry, realising that Roscoff has surprised me. I will make a return visit one day.

Lovestruck in Leningrad

Aside glance at the uniform and its occupant, the young Russian officer sitting next to me at the Moscow State Circus, was all it took. It was love at first sight. A totally unplanned event in my tourist itinerary.

It was the mid-1980s, time of Perestroika and Glasnost, wonderfully evocative words which had entered the English language overnight even if we weren't entirely sure what they meant. Gorbachev was in charge, and I was in Leningrad, as St Petersburg was then called, on a city visit meticulously managed by Intourist, the Soviet tour operator. I travelled there across the Baltic Sea by boat from Stockholm—an overnight crossing to Helsinki with a coachload of Swedes. Onboard we dined on smörgåsbord, a fitting choice, and had enjoyed a romantic sailing through the small pine-capped islands of the Swedish and Finnish archipelagos at dusk and dawn respectively. It was a propitious start.

In Helsinki, we transferred to a coach and drove towards the Finnish-Russian border. The landscape began to change as soon as we left the bright lights of central Helsinki. Block after block of grey monotone apartments caused me to nod off and for the next hour or so my head lolled uncomfortably against the pleated curtain of the coach window. When I woke, we had reached the border and were being ordered off so that our visas could be scrutinised and the coach thoroughly searched for the contraband that we were undoubtedly smuggling into Russia to sell on the black market. It hadn't occurred to me to bring cigarettes or spirits to subsidise my trip and I was rather disappointed when the Russian border guards' search failed to reveal anything concealed by my fellow passengers either. We should then have been waved on our way, but Soviet protocol demanded otherwise. The coach was cranked up on a vehicle lift so that its underside could be checked – presumably for more contraband rather than to inspect its roadworthiness. Some time later we were grudgingly allowed back on the federal highway to Leningrad, a mere 250 miles away—just a Lilliputian footstep into the sprawling expanse of Russia. There were no further stops.

Over the next two days we 'got to know' Leningrad, enjoying the officially sanctioned experience that we were given by our Soviet hosts. Every morning after breakfast, the red and white tour bus and its glum driver were waiting outside the hotel. Our guide, unsmiling in her ill-fitting grey Intourist uniform would bid us 'Good morning' and then wrestle with the crackling on-board microphone as we settled into our seats for that day's magical mystery tour. We referred to it as a mystery tour because no advance programme was available although it did become possible to predict some regular features of the daily tour. Usually included was some instruction in the government buildings of Leningrad and their bureaucratic functions. I tried hard to concentrate but am not sure how many of the salient details I retained.

The tours of the squares were a bit easier as each was crowned with the statue of an important historical figure. I successfully identified the first one as Lenin. The next one may have been Lenin too. It was a bit confusing as several appeared to have been cast from the same mould from the neck downwards. All adopted a similar dramatic stance—in mid stride and scowling into the distance. Their coats were invariably flung open—I decided that this must be an allusion to the formidable winds of the Russian steppes—and an arm, usually the right one, was outstretched. At the end of the arm there was often an accusative finger—which seemed to be pointing at me. A sense of guilt crept over me with each new statue we saw. I was relieved when the guide informed us that they were pointing out the future path to economic prosperity.

Government buildings and Soviet squares aside, the tours did contain some anticipated sights. There was a memorable visit to the Hermitage Museum and its huge collection of art and cultural artefacts, and an evening drive along the Nevsky Prospekt, the city's most famous street, lit up along its entire length. There was also an unexpected stop at an orthodox church. Good, I thought. We're going to see some icons. I entered, expecting a candlelit interior heavy with incense and walls adorned with devotional paintings of saints, whose penetrating eyes meet yours wherever you are standing. At last, we would see something from the pre-communist era, a taste of the old Russia and maybe even a glimpse into the Slavic soul.

But sadly, there were no icons and not a whiff of incense. The building was no longer functioning as a church and was instead housing the Museum of the History of Religion and its dusty display cases.

Things began to look up on the last night of our tour. The guide proudly informed us that as a special treat we had a choice for our final evening's entertainment. We could choose to see a performance of the Bolshoi Ballet—which came highly recommended by our guide—or see the Moscow State Circus. Unaccustomed to treats or a choice, many of our group vacillated wildly between the possibilities but were eventually persuaded to choose the Bolshoi. Three of us decided on the circus. Our tour guide was displeased as this meant organising two separate sets of tickets as well as minders to escort us. Being both non-compliant and in the minority, the circus goers took second place in the arrangements and so we arrived at the venue late.

Everyone was already seated and the show had just begun. In the very full auditorium there were no free places together so we were separated and quickly distributed to three empty seats. The minder ushered me to one in the middle of a back row. No one was happy about the disturbance. 'Izvinitje, izvinitje,' I excused myself as I squeezed along the narrow line ejecting several Russian families from their seats in the process, and trampling on the food and drink they had carefully arranged on the floor in front of them. I reached my place, sat down and it was then that I turned to flash an apologetic smile at my handsome neighbour. He was looking straight ahead.

The circus did not disappoint. Act after act bewitched us. A troupe of clowns poured out into the ring and began to juggle, then pushed and pulled each other around in slapstick fashion to loud encouragement from the younger members of the audience. Then followed a band of Cossacks in their wide trousers and flapping tunics. They stood astride their galloping horses and whirled themselves dangerously over the saddles or hung by a hand from the flanks of their mounts as they dashed around in circles. There was a collective holding of breath as trapeze artists performed gravity-defying acrobatics with split second timing and caught each other in mid-air.

Something also caught my attention in the aisle. It was a large round spotlight anchored to the floor and focused on the stage. Behind it sat a babushka, a rotund Russian grandmother complete with headscarf. She was the spotlight operator. Every so often she laid down her knitting and flicked a switch or changed the angle of the spotlight.

But recalling it decades later, one memory eclipsed all of this. The handsome young Russian officer sitting at my side. Immaculate in every respect in his pine green uniform, I surreptitiously admired each detail: from the embossed brass buttons on his jacket to the impressive high-peaked cap with black visor, carefully positioned on his lap. On the green band that encircled its brim there was an emblematic red star set on a gold badge. Unable to resist, I took a quick peek at his profile and noted the carefully combed fair hair curling against his forehead and his clear blue eyes, shining with enjoyment. In that instance, I was smitten. Perhaps I had been intoxicated by the excitement of the circus or just captivated by a man in uniform. It didn't matter. Here beside me was the face of the real Russia I'd been looking for. But I could only idolise from afar. We neither spoke, nor exchanged a meaningful look. So dear reader, I regret to say that I did not marry him. In fact, I never saw him again. Unlike me, he only had eyes for the circus.

Seeing Red in the Canary Islands

T**reading** carefully to avoid slipping, I follow the zigzag path down the steep hillside of Barranco de Guiniguada into the ravine of the botanic garden of Gran Canaria. It's late September. Most plants have finished flowering and look tired and scruffy. Their rejuvenation in the spring time is still a long way off.

No flowers then, but I pause to admire the palms, which come in all shapes and sizes here including the body-builder of all palms—Mister muscle-bound, the endemic Dragon Tree. In one grove, several specimens of this tree stand erect, displaying a ring of sausage-shaped branches which support the palm's dense green canopy.

Further along the path, I arrive at a bridge, straddling a gorge, where a sign informs me that the giant Gran Canarian lizard is also present. I lean over and spy one, peeping out from a rocky crevice. It's a dark monster, prehistoric-looking but, fortunately, vegetarian. Another one is splayed out on the rock face. It's a sheer drop down into the gorge but the lizard looks relaxed, defying gravity with claws that grip like superglue.

I walk on, my interest aroused. I sense that another discovery is imminent. It comes in a dry grove of prickly pear cactus.

Some are strangely white and a transfixing sight. An ethereal Christmas scene of seemingly snow-clad cacti.

Prickly pear cacti were brought to southern Europe and the Canary islands from their native habitat in the Americas and cultivated for their edible tunera or pears. Here they stand with their flat lateral stems stretching awkwardly outwards. Resembling fleshy lobes, they are studded with protective spines—the reduced 'leaves' of the cactus.

I move closer, trying to avoid the lethal spines, so that I can examine the white stuff decorating them. An early frost, perhaps? I insert my fingers and take a pinch. No, it's a mysterious white powder and something else. It contains some tiny oval bugs. Squashed with my thumb they spurt a vibrant red slash of colour: bright vermillion 'blood'.

A vague memory of something I have read about the Canary Isles surfaces in my brain and the mystery is solved. Coccineal—the source of carmine dye since ancient times. These are female coccineal bugs. Living in colonies while feeding on cactus sap, they secrete waxy snow-white fibres to protect themselves from the sun's heat.

Europeans crossing to the Americas first learned from the Aztecs about using cochineal as a dye for cloth and an important trade began. In their home region, the bugs are still cultivated in prickly pear plantations. In Peru they are harvested, dried and still used as food dye in sweets and confectionery and colourant in cosmetic products including lipstick and eye shadow.

But to produce even a small quantity of dye, tens of thousands of dried insects need to be boiled so that their bodies release carminic acid, which is then mixed with chemicals to give the dye its long lasting quality.

On Gran Canaria, coccineal production has all but disappeared with the rise of synthetic dyes but in the 1800s, not far from here, the town of Arucas grew prosperous from coccineal. Now only a few local artisans continue collecting the bugs to dye their knitting yarn and fabric naturally.

After that first time in the botanic garden, I encounter the coccineal bug often. On wasteland and roadsides across Gran Canaria. Wherever the prickly pear cactus colonises, the insect follows its food plant. And seeing them again, the memory of that first vermillion streak on my fingers returns.

A Hitchhiker's Guide
to the Bay of Biscay

The continental ferry bobbed about, large though it was, like a geographically challenged rubber duck. We were crossing the Bay of Biscay, heading towards the north coast of Spain—in a haphazard sort of way. Our ship was three hours behind schedule: the emergency evacuation of a sick passenger had taken it off course and towards France so that a helicopter could reach us. Now the tail end of Storm Lorenzo was whipping us on towards our intended destination.

Up on deck ten, our small group of whale watchers huddled together, swaying slowly in unison with the vessel. We might have been football supporters performing a Mexican wave but for our waterproofs and the binoculars pressed firmly to our faces as we scoured the sea around us. We were here for a purpose: volunteering our time to survey whales near the continental shelf where the Atlantic Ocean plummets unimaginable fathoms into deep dark canyons below. Down there the whales fed, occasionally surfacing to fill their giant lungs with air before plunging down again. We had made a few sightings, a blow of white spray or forceful waterspout in the distance. But the creatures themselves had been harder to see and identify. When they broke surface, unruly whipped-up waves, white and frothy, shielded their backs and dorsal fins from our probing eyes.

'Coming for a coffee?' my cabin mate asked, clasping binoculars in hands blotchy with cold, as her black beanie hat dripped rainwater onto the deck between us. 'I'll join you in a bit,' I answered. I was still hankering after something more. She left.

Turning back to the sea, with elbows propped on the ship's rail, I raised my binoculars again, gradually becoming mesmerised by the slate-grey waves, unceasing and unstill. Half an hour passed before I eventually closed my aching eyes and looked away. The image of the churning seascape stayed with me as I refocussed on my companions. Only three of us remained now. The warm coffee lounge had lured the rest of the group inside. Above us, a lumpy grey blanket of cloud lay untidily across much of the sky. But the rain had finally stopped and a small corner of the blanket was turned down like a bed ready to climb into. A blue triangle was visible. I watched as the opening grew bigger and a stream of sunlight forced its way through to dance across the sea surface. The waves became calmer and settled into a gentler rhythm, while around me, patches of dry deck began to appear. I exchanged a gratified smile with my fellow whale watchers.

Suddenly, a shout rang out and a hand pointed energetically. Not at the sea, but behind us towards the deck on the port side of the ship. At first I could see nothing but the drying deck in front of me. Then a very small dark object entered my field of vision. It was moving erratically through the air. Drawing nearer, I could see a tiny torpedo-like body jerkily moving over the deck towards us and emitting a strange buzzing noise as its wings beat rapidly. My mind jumped back and forth without conviction: Not a bird? A bee then? No. Maybe a humming-bird? Not quite.

'Hummingbird hawk moth,' my neighbour, an expert entomologist, informed me with some satisfaction. 'Autumn migrant. Could be making for Spain or even North Africa.' A migrant, so this unlikely insect, a miniature Cuban cigar with wings, was making the long and hazardous journey to a warmer clime. Earlier in the year thousands of its kind had made their way in the opposite direction to spend their summer sucking up nectar from buddleia and honeysuckle in English gardens. Their rapid wingbeat with its audible hum enabled them to hover in mid-air as they probed flowers with their long proboscis.

Our ship must have been a welcome stopover for this fellow traveller and might have brought it closer to its destination. Transfixed, I watched as our enterprising hitchhiker veered away, still humming loudly and came down to rest somewhere on the stern of the vessel. But it was not alone. From then on we were visited by a stream of other creatures in transit, all hitching a ride as we made our way across the Bay of Biscay. A short-eared owl accompanied us for several hours, sometimes scrutinising other passengers severely as it perched on the railing or circled, observing us from above. Also making the long migration south was a convoy of small birds. The excited twitchers on deck called them out by name as they flew in:

chiffchaff, wheatear, meadow pipit, a robin, even a tiny gold-crest—all on the move southwards. The deck became quite crowded with avian guests as they competed for landing space and a quiet corner in which to have a quick preen, freshen up and regain strength.

I didn't see the hummingbird hawk moth again. After resting a while, it must have resumed its journey. Soon a dark line appeared on the horizon signalling land, and ahead of us a straggle of Spanish fishing vessels could be seen, making their way slowly back to port with the night's catch. I had a hunch I knew where our hitchhiker might be heading to pick up its next ride.

A Ride into the Shadow Underworld

'Halloo Mrs. Where you go? You wan' becak?' The Indonesian pedicab driver hails me, having pedalled up unnoticed behind his unwitting victim in this dusty backstreet.

'No, thanks. Jalan, jalan (I'm walking),' I reply, quickening my pace. But in the sultry heat of a tropical afternoon, my tired and weak legs are no match for his brown sinewy ones, and he is not going to be put off that easily.

I am in Jogja, as the locals affectionately call the royal city of Yogyakarta. It lies in the central province of Java 550 kilometres east of Jakarta, and I'm taking a meandering route across the Indonesian archipelago, eastwards towards the islands of Bali and Lombok, seeing the sights as I go. Jogja is my halfway point.

Two days ago, feeling intrepid, I struggled up to the summit of nearby Mount Merapi, a smoking and volatile volcano, to see the sun rise over its fiery crater. Shooting stars accompanied me, dancing across the night sky. Below in the rich volcanic soil, field upon field of pungent tobacco plants grew. I had walked through them on my way to the volcano, feeling giddy and intoxicated by their overpowering scent. After the climb, the young boy guiding us back down had gently made fun of us as we stumbled along the path of lava fragments, losing our foothold on the scree. Giggling, he pointed to our legs and mimicked with his fingers, commenting, 'You walk like ant now.' So for the next two days I'm recovering my strength and dignity, and simply hanging loose in Jogja.

Just now, I have to admit I don't have a clue where I am in this clutter of small lookalike streets so I decide that resistance is not only futile but also counterproductive. I give in and accept the offer of a becak ride.

'Okay. To the Kraton Sultan's Palace, silhakan (please).' I clasp the strut supporting the flimsy roof of the vehicle and climb in, collapsing onto the hot plastic seat behind the driver. Five minutes of no-sweat peddle power later (I am a light load), he drops me in a courtyard in front of the red-roofed palace and I pay up. I am surprised when he hands me a scrappy bit of paper in return. His business card maybe? No. Peering at it, I see that it's an illegible address, scribbled in fading biro.

'You like Wayang kulit? Jogja famous. Bagus (Very good). You come see. Seven o'clock. Special price for you.' He grins, taking my non-committal shrug as agreement, then he pedals off to find another customer.

That evening I surprise myself and follow up on the invitation. Indecipherable though it is to me, the piece of paper holds no coded enigma for the next becak driver. I find him sleeping in the back of his vehicle outside Guest House Hibiscus where I'm staying. We set off. Rattling over the dark potholed street, the becak shakes me about like a bean in a tin can and with each new jolt I wonder if I have made the right decision. The unlit house where I am deposited twenty minutes later does not look particularly welcoming or even inhabited. For the second time that day, I have no idea where I am.

'Here Mrs. This place. Terima kasih (Thank you).' And he too peddles away. It does not feel quite right. I hesitate in front of the entrance—a small porch with a broken roof and steps that lead down to a wooden door. It's closed. There is no sound from inside. It doesn't resemble any of the usual tourist venues. Suddenly, the door swings open; a draped mosquito net parts and a woman's arm extends and pulls me forward, 'Salamat datang! Welcome! Wayang kulit, yes? Please come.'

I follow her and we descend more steps into a basement. Yes, I am here for Wayang kulit, Indonesian shadow puppet theatre, a recommended cultural highlight of any visit to Jogja. And I see that I'm not alone. The basement is bursting with an audience in waiting. A faint smell of sweat hangs over the dark room and the eyes in the faces of the twenty or so people sitting cross-legged on its floor are alight with expectation. Indonesian devotees of this ancient art sit alongside curious foreigners. I find a small space and crouch down, arranging my legs into a comfortable position.

In front of us stands a large white canvas screen, backlit and empty. To the left sits an orchestra—a line of four gamelan players, all men, dressed in traditional batik jackets, sarongs and headdress. They sit, calm and poised before their instruments ready to provide the music to accompany the show. I can see bronze gongs and cymbals of varying sizes, a xylophone, a leather-topped drum and a bamboo flute.

I am looking around at my fellow spectators when a hush suddenly descends on the room. The music starts up. It is immediately strange. A jangling and discordant sound. I concentrate, trying to discern a rhythm but the chimes and bongs assault my unaccustomed westerner's ears.

Then a shrill commanding voice replaces the music and the shadow profiles of two stick-like human figures with bulbous heads move slowly across the screen towards each other. The performance has begun. The puppet handlers kneel behind, out of sight below the screen, and dexterously manipulate the rods attached to their puppets' long skinny limbs. The figures shake and quiver into life. Beaky-nosed and bulging-eyed characters, they are hunched and grotesque. These are the stuff of nightmares. I have read that they are based on stories from ancient Hindu epics which the storyteller embellishes with political, humorous or philosophical twists to delight his domestic audience. The puppets are all equipped with long menacing fingers that wave and point as the story unfolds. Some represent fools or heroes; others strange gods or demons, but I am the stranger here and cannot tell the good guys from the bad guys. I watch in wonder, buoyed along by the jerking shadows and the jarring music but comprehending nothing. I am uncertain where all this will lead and lost without translation. It is another becak ride into the unknown.

Time passes, the shadow puppets come and go. There are interactions between them but I cannot tell whether they reflect harmony or conflict. Without warning, the music starts to gain momentum and I sense we are reaching the climax. It culminates in a clanging crescendo and stops, dead. The drama is over. On the screen, the villain has been dispatched and all that is left is a fallen shadow with the victorious hero bending over him, or so I surmise. I may be wrong. The puppet master and his assistants step out from behind the screen and take a bow. One of them I know. It is my first driver from earlier that day. Becak driver by day, puppet handler by night. Silently, the audience files out and climbs the steps. At the door the draped mosquito net parts again and the woman bids us 'Selamat Malam (Good night),' as we are released from this netherworld. It feels strangely liberating to breathe the warm evening air again.

The Mystery of a Nudge in the Night

E very three or four years there is a population explo-
sion. In 1994 there was one, and I know this because
I was there.

On summer nights, where the Arctic Circle severs the neck
of Norway like a guillotine, the world is bathed in a mysterious
twilight. Sleep does not come naturally here. Around midnight,
in a forest next to a surging river, I tossed and turned, blaming
my restlessness on the tent—erected hastily, the ground, lumpy,
and my sleeping bag constricting me like an anaconda. The
world outside was awake and disturbed too. I gave up wrestling
with the sleep angel and lay, listening to its sounds. My back felt
uncomfortable and suddenly twitched. Once and then twice I
felt a small shove; a clearly discernible nudge, from below. Too
gentle and subtle for an earth tremor, but what then? A mole or
a mouse burrowing beneath me perhaps? The nudging stopped.
I turned on my side, pulled the sleeping bag up over my ears.
The sleep angel won, and I finally drifted off to the sound of the
muffled roar of the river.

The next morning the natural world was alive and bright at
an unsociably early hour. The rich tang of damp forest humus
filled the air. Scrambling out of the tent I set off to collect a few
bilberries to pep up my morning porridge. When I returned,

my companions were up and boiling water for tea. Over breakfast we planned the day's walk through the forest. We packed
up the tents and brushed out the previous day's accumulated
bits of twig and leaf from our socks and boots. Then we were
on our way.

The path we had chosen wound its way through a tangle of
trees and over lumps and bumps created by ancient Caledonian
rocks bulging out from the earth. Small thickets of robust bilberry lined the route, cheering us on with their red and green
bunting-like leaves and irresistible berries. It wasn't long before
our hands and mouths were stained purple.

After an hour or so we paused for a break and took out our
water bottles. Birdsong was coming from a tree nearby. Rummaging in our packs, we found our binoculars and scanned
the branches to locate its source. I was startled by an abrupt
movement at my side. It was my companion's head, jerking
downwards in surprise to look at the path. My gaze followed. A
colourful furry bundle tumbled over his boot and disappeared
into a bilberry thicket. We bent down and peered deep into the
bush. At ground level, our faces were met by a high-pitched
screech and then the small bundle mock-charged us. Its tiny
black eyes glittered with rage and a set of equally small yellow
incisors bared up at us from an angry open mouth. This unexpected display of feistiness took us by surprise. I was still trying
to decide what I was looking at when my companion exclaimed
in delight, 'it's a lemming.'

Unimpressed by us or my friend's identification skills,
our plucky foe backed into the security of the bilberries, still

screeching and bearing its fangs at us. With two goliaths bar-
ring its way out, it realized it was in a tight corner and decided
that making itself scarce was the better part of valour. The bush
trembled a couple of times as a lemming in a hurry negotiated
its interior, seeking an alternative exit. Then suddenly the bundle shot out and away into the forest. It was gone.

This was the first of many encounters we had with members
of the Lemmus lemmus species that summer holiday. They ran,
leapt, danced or sauntered across our path everywhere. Sometimes they froze in front of us, hoping to go unnoticed. For
every lemming we saw, no doubt a further twenty were hiding
nearby waiting to dash across the path. All were lemmings on a
mission, driven by a need, an urge, a message communicated on
the lemming bush telegraph—who knows how, but they knew.
Going where lemmings had gone before; they were following
the example of lemming communities since, well, the dawn of
lemmings communities.

Lemmus lemmus or the Norwegian lemming is a ham-
ster-like rodent related to voles. I discovered that it has many
exotic cousins with intriguing names such as the bog lemming;
the wood lemming, the Steppe lemming and, the Arctic lemming, which turns white in winter. Lemmus lemmus, is, how-
ever, the 'true' lemming, the one known for its periodic mass
migrations or so-called suicide runs.

From our many meetings that summer I got to know the
creature well, both temperamentally and physically. Although
smaller in size, its coloration reminded me of a scruffy pet
guinea-pig I once owned: black, ginger and white. It wears

these three colours in a rather untidy tufty coat that appears to have seen better days. Beneath the overcoat are four stubby but surprisingly agile little legs and a short tail. Explosions of its population occur every few years when its numbers increase to a point where there is insufficient food for all. And so their only option is to migrate en masse in search of new territory. They travel by day, but also by night. Now I understood that mysterious nudge in the night; it was a lemming on the move, passing beneath my tent and attempting to shove me out of the way. This was going to be a useful conversation starter for a dinner party one day. I also found out that lemmings not only migrate over land but they can also swim across lakes and rivers. Oceans pose a bigger problem so lemmings that leap off cliff edges are not suicidal but have just taken a wrong turn somewhere along the way.

That explosive summer of 1994 I fraternized a lot with the lemming population and felt rather privileged to have witnessed this remarkable event for myself!

Birdsong

I turn a corner and there it is: Aureli's bar in Via Quattro Fontane, the street of the four fountains. Just a few steps away is the junction with a busy main road, which as usual is shrouded in hazy floating ribbons of sunlight intermingled with traffic fumes. A stream of dusty Fiats and whining Vespas weaves alongside the departing orange caterpillar bus that I have just stepped off. At the bus stop there is the sudden hissing release of air from another bus, as its concertina doors jerk open. Passengers spill out while new ones surge inside. Arms and bodies collide, squeezing together like pasta shapes being strained into a bowl. A momentary fusion of soft bodies in bus doorways, which is normal here; the queue is not an Italian custom. I walk on towards my destination.

As I push open the glass door of Aureli's entrance, the wafting aroma of roasted coffee beans immediately greets my nostrils. I breathe in deeply, satisfied. The bar is full of customers. Coffee is the life blood of Italian society. I am hailed from a distance by one of the barista. Very little evades the sharp eyes of Franco. He recognises me as one of the bar's regulars, a profesoressa inglese from the language school across the street. With both hands on the chrome coffee making machine, he simultaneously prepares two cappuccios and an espresso, while acknowledging me.

I feel welcome. Through the throng of people, I catch a second fleeting glimpse of Franco's starched white apron and rolled shirt sleeves as plumes of hot milk steam billow upwards. Marco, another barista, is nearby, emptying the indefatigable dishwasher, and stacking cups, saucers and glasses ready for the next batch of customers. I wade into the sea of people and ease myself through to the till where I order my coffee and pay. With scontrino in hand—my proof of purchase, I'm on my way to the counter when I recognise some of my students talking animatedly at a table in the corner. They are too engrossed to notice me. No doubt, not discussing today's homework but perhaps the latest political scandal to rock Italy. I see one of them throw his hands up in mock irony over a copy of La Repubblica, the daily newspaper. Another's face bears that 'knowing' cynical expression, which all Italians are born with.

I finally reach the counter and ostentatiously put down my scontrino, intending it to be seen. On the floor below, the first wave of breakfasting Italians have left behind the flakes of their cornetti and the screwed-up balls of their paper napkins. I wait to be served. But today the barista breezes past me to serve another. I continue waiting, trying to catch his eye. The bar is busy today. My fingers play with the receipt and on impulse, I hold it up like a small flag. I stand like this, unnoticed, but watch as the person on either side of me is served. Frustration and then anxiety bubble up inside me. My class begins soon and there is still photocopying to do.

It's almost as if am not even here. Forgotten by the barista. The people, who were around me, are all fading away and the bar suddenly seems empty and quieter. What's that? It sounds like a bird singing somewhere. Something has happened. Perhaps it's the lull before the lunchtime rush. Surely, he'll see and serve me now. He approaches at last.

My mouth anticipates the first frothy sip of a warm cappuccino. But the barista melts away behind the counter. I watch, puzzled, as his torso, then apron and gesticulating hands mysteriously dissolve until only his face hangs wavering in front of me like a Cheshire cat. His mouth moves, voicing inaudible words. I cannot hear him but only the sound of that bird singing somewhere nearby.

The people have all vanished and Aureli's bar too. I am alone but where? Sitting in a chair, here, in my garden. I can still hear the birdsong but there is no-one else. Recollection of the stark reality of the present floods in to fill the vacuum left in my head. I'm in a lockdown world; a coronavirus one with its social privations. For a brief moment my daydream transported me back to a place I inhabited some thirty years ago. A joyful dive into the rich tapestry of Italian life—close-up and personal, greeting and touching, sharing airspace, immersed in the social fabric of daily life. The antithesis of now. Now, I am alone, pondering where that world has gone, and wondering if it will ever return.

The Village of Cloves

The clapped-out old bemo, Indonesia's version of the minibus, rattles to a stop near a dirt track leading to the clove village, and we climb out. It has been a rough ride to get here. Cheap enough but a skeleton-shaking fairground experience. We stand for a moment in the sun, savouring the sensation of immobility while our bones settle back into their rightful places. We have travelled here from Manado, the northern capital of Sulawesi, one of Indonesia's largest islands, exotically shaped like a butterfly on the map. Visiting a rural clove plantation sounded like a good way to escape the hustle of the city for a while.

After a swig or two of warm water from our bottles, we start walking slowly towards the cluster of low buildings in the distance. The fields that line the track have already been harvested of their crop; maybe maize, it's hard to say, as only some patchwork stubble remains. Feeling stickily hot, and with our ears assaulted by the buzzing of unseen insects, we walk on in the afternoon haze. A field rat, nose to the ground, is caught off-guard. It dashes away, leaping in panic across the clumps of stubble. As we approach the village, we raise our own noses and sniff the air. There is a pervasive sweet smell. Faint but familiar. It must be the cloves.

The time for their harvest is now. Cloves, the aromatic flower buds of an evergreen tree belonging to the Myrtle family, are being plucked by hand before they open; then laid out to dry in the sun. It's a family-run operation that we have come to watch and it's recommended in our guidebook.

When we reach the outskirts of the village we pause to drink more water. The scent is stronger here and yet there are no clove trees in sight. Occupying the corner of the field, there is only a dilapidated bamboo structure complete with a caved-in roof. We are drawn towards it. Its contents are shielded by the broken bamboo fence but there is space enough to squeeze through a hole. The air inside is thick with the sweet smell. But where is it coming from? Inside a colony of plants is growing unrestrained. Neglected it seems, they have been left to fend for themselves. So, in wild abandon they have climbed like rampant voluptuous vines all over the light-dappled shady interior. Some have fleshy yellow-green flowers; others have gone to seed and dangle green pods, long and lush. That fragrant smell: now I know—it's vanilla. These are vanilla orchids. Not abandoned, but being cultivated in this place for their pods.

Delighted with our find, we take photographs, all the time drinking in their heady perfume. Eventually, we clamber out through the bamboo fence again, sated, and with our senses still reeling from the botanical orgy inside.

At the village entrance we are met by a young boy. We greet him, a little guiltily, hoping he didn't see us emerging from the hole in the bamboo fence. 'Selamat pagi (Good day).'

'Hello Mister. Apa kabar? (How are you?),' he greets us in return. Then, 'You like orchid?'

We smile in what we hope is a non-committal way. But it's no good. He already knows everything.

'Please, you see,' he beckons. And we follow obediently to the village and into one of the huts. There lying criss-crossed on the floor are heaps of vanilla pods, some freshly picked and still green; others shrivelled, blackish and ready to sell on to a middle man. Two women in faded sarongs squat on their haunches on the floor, one older and gap-toothed; the other a shy young girl; they are sorting and laying out the pods in batches. We watch in silence, feeling that we are intruding but the boy has us in his charge. Soon we are taking photos of the process, and even the shy girl is persuaded to pose with a vanilla pod while we take her picture.

Before we leave, I produce a few rupiahs, and a dark vanilla pod is handed to me. The young boy oversees the transaction, beaming. Afterwards, he accompanies us to the edge of the village, self-assured in his role as visitor guide. We thank him and as an afterthought, I try to enquire about the cloves but receive only a puzzled look from him. His engaging grin returns. He has no knowledge of what 'cloves' means but senses that we are satisfied with the vanilla orchids. It seems we may have got the wrong village. Perhaps the result of a misunderstanding with the driver who brought us here. On the ride back, as we are jolted up and down on the hard bemo seats, we laugh, amused by the serendipity of our ill-fated plan to visit the village of cloves.

The Misadventure of a Goose

A candle flickers: an eye, a chin, a cheekbone; parts of faces become illuminated briefly. They belong to a group of pilgrims, seated in a huddle around a low table; in front of them a circle of beers from which they take occasional sips. They are exchanging stories, straining to understand dialects and accents, which seem strange and incomprehensible to each other.

No, it is not medieval times but 2017. These modern-day pilgrims are gathered in a pub in the small village of Walsingham, a place lost in the heart of Norfolk. They are Weegies, they inform me. In other words, Glaswegians. They are resilient people with a unique sense of humour and a love of bantering, I discover. Travelling down from the far north of the country, they have driven in turn without stopping. I have travelled up from the other end of the country, an island off the south coast, taking a less demanding if more complicated option—a route involving a boat, a train, the Tube, a train again and then several local buses—to reach this place in the wilds of East Anglia. Like them, I have made a pilgrimage here.

I have come on an impulsive decision made in November. It is a solo venture and neither an obvious time of year nor a typical destination for today's pilgrim. Every year people flock in their hundreds of thousands to the pilgrimage hotspots of Rome and Jerusalem and in springtime many more walk the now re-popularised el camino routes which criss-cross the whole of Europe to converge at Santiago de Compostela in Spain. An antipathy for crowds, heavy backpacks and blisters has made me set my sights somewhat lower, on a location half-buried here in the fen country in the now barren brown fields of north Norfolk.

A few days ago I conducted a quick google search, then, with a strong magnifying glass found this tiny spot on the map. I realised that mid-November was the perfect time to come. The weather could be relied upon to be unreliable and I would avoid any possible encounters with a crowd. I rejected the idea of walking there, to avoid blisters. Robert Louis Stevenson went sojourning across France on a donkey and Che Guevara rode a motorbike across Latin America. Even if I wasn't following the perambulating example of the Canterbury pilgrims or John Bunyan's protagonist, my challenge would be tackling the cross-country transport system in the UK instead.

So I fill a small backpack—a suitcase doesn't seem to fit the image—and go online to buy a train ticket as far as Norwich. Then I check the timetables and set off on the start of my own pilgrim's progress.

In Norwich I discover that there is no direct bus service to Walsingham, and confusingly, there are two Walsinghams— Little Walsingham and Great Walsingham. 'Which one do you want?' the first of several bus drivers inquires of me in his smooth dipthong-less Norfolk accent. I make a choice. It doesn't matter as fortunately they are not far apart—I will walk between them if necessary.

Several bus changes and many scenic village stops later, and with darkness falling, the last bus sets me down at a small triangular intersection, the centre of Little Walsingham, and I wander down the only street, a short stretch of timber-framed buildings, to look for my accommodation. I find the Pilgrim Hostel, register, and leaving my backpack in the reception office, cross a small courtyard to join the dinner queue in the refectory. There is hardly need of a queue but I join the end behind four talkative Glaswegians. It turns out that they are old hands at doing pilgrimages. This is the second day of their third trip to the shrines of Walsingham. I am very impressed.

Discovering that I am a total novice in the art of pilgrimage, they take me under their wing and over dinner instruct me as we slowly break through the language barrier. I learn about a Saxon chapel and a Holy House; the ruins of an Augustinian Priory, an ancient Marian shrine created from the vision of a noblewoman; visited and venerated for several hundred years in medieval England and as famous then as Rome and Jerusalem. Believers made long and arduous journeys on foot from all over England and farther afield to reach it. I am filled with awe as it dawns on me how many feet have trodden this way before mine. The search for spiritual meaning, purification, a fresh start drove tens of thousands of people to Walsingham down the ages before eventually its statue and buildings were torn down and burnt during the Reformation. For the next few centuries the village and the ruins of its historic past slept undisturbed until, once again, the faithful began to visit it in the twentieth century. But I am still imagining those medieval pilgrims, trudging a thousand footpaths across the landscape to pour into this small village from all directions. Inspired by my dinner companions, I begin planning. Tomorrow I will don my walking boots and head out across the dank and windy fields to follow the old Pilgrim's Way and visit the outlying shrines. And, like those before me, I will take home a souvenir pilgrim's badge as my tangible proof of visit.

We continue talking as we eat and are just starting the pudding course when it happens. Abruptly, we are plunged into darkness. Pilgrimages, ancient and modern must meet such hazards so we sit and wait, unfazed. Technology rescues us. Mobile phones are pulled out of pockets to shed light on our apple crumble and custard. Someone goes off to look for a fusebox. Coffee follows and our conversation flows out into the darkness. A box of handy devotional candles appears and soon a myriad of small lights adorn the refectory. Then a news update passes from table to table. It seems that fiddling with the fusebox has not solved the problem and someone has noticed that the lights are out in the entire village and even in the surrounding ones too. It's quite possible that normal service will not be resumed that night. Taking up our candles, we tentatively step outside to experience this new world steeped in darkness. There is little to see at ground level but above in the spangled autumn sky, the solicitous stars gaze down on us from their distant thrones. We feel small and insignificant, perhaps as did earlier visitors to the shrine. A reverential silence engulfs us as the universe awes us with its magnificent presence.

Humbled and slightly uncertain, we stand close together; wondering what to do next. Someone makes a Glaswegian joke to break the eerie black silence. I don't get it but then I didn't catch all the words. Someone else hits on the pilgrim's answer to all dilemmas sent to test, and we follow him in a stumbling, candlelit procession down to the pub at the street's intersection. Many of the villagers are there already. Candles are on every table and the hand-pumped beer is flowing. Gladdened by the company, we while away the next few hours, grappling with the task of human communication through our different vernaculars. Then with last orders called, we again form a ragged line and, with dripping candles, return to the hostel to finger-feel our way along the corridor walls to our rooms.

I wake in the morning and tentatively flick a switch. The lights come on as if nothing has happened. Power has been restored during the night. And what caused it? The engineers report that a migrating goose flew into an overhead power line, taking out the supply to a cluster of Norfolk villages and cooking itself to a crisp in the process. The Glaswegians and I part company after breakfast, they to start the long drive back to Scotland and me to find the Pilgrim's Way. They ask me if I think I will return one day and I reply a little ruefully, 'Well, perhaps. It's too early to tell.' But I am already wondering what can possibly surpass the memory of last night. The candlelit procession to share a beer with new companions from a faraway place, all brought about by the misadventure of an errant goose.

The Last Wood Turner

Captured in a shaft of sunlight in the doorway, a spiral of fine dust was slowly dancing; recreating the harmony of the spheres. Outside in the narrow, cobbled street, I stopped to admire it in childlike wonder. A whiff of sweet resin tickled my nostrils—newly sawn pine wood—the scent drew me closer. I was feeling hot and weary, having lost my way in the winding backstreets of Toledo. The open doorway was inviting.

The interior was dark and my eyes took time to adjust. An elaborate small cage, entirely constructed of wood, stood on a table just inside the entrance. On parallel perches facing each other, sat two goldfinches. They had seen better days; scrawny, but with bright eyes alert in their scarlet masks, they observed me, observing them.

'Son mis amigos: Chico y Chica (They are my friends: Boy and Girl).' A disembodied voice informed me, adding that they were eleven years old. Eleven years old? Incredulous that such a tiny bird could live so long, I turned towards the source of the voice. It belonged to Luis, Tornero y Artesano de la Madera, a traditional wood turner and artisan, whose workshop I had entered.

He stepped out of the darkness in a work apron, his shirt sleeves rolled to the elbow, the hairs on his forearms coated in amber-coloured wood dust. Surrounding us was a cornucopia of woodcraft—chairs, hat-racks, candlesticks, table legs, spinning tops, doorstops, even a church monstrance. Luis had made them all with his woodturning machine.

'Ha hecho muchas cosas (You've made a lot),' I said, looking around slightly disoriented as I tried to take stock of everything.

It was a family business, passed down through grandfather and father—abuelo y padre—and finally to Luis himself, now nearly fifty years in the trade, he said proudly.

'Y sus hijos? (And your sons)' I enquired. No, there was no-one else to take it on, he explained. In two years' time everything would be gone. He gestured emphatically sweeping his work-worn hands in front of him, splaying their cracked fingers. The work is hard and bad for the eyes. He paused before continuing and I noticed one of his pale grey eyes squinting slightly leftwards. Sometimes the concentration leaves you feeling crazy at the end of the day. Now there was only him left but he was proud to be the last of his profession still working in Toledo.

Then, in a matter of fact voice: I don't make much money. The tourists want things cheaper or just take photos. They don't understand how many hours it takes to make something. I stroked the curved neck of a wooden heron and nodded, staying silent. Only he was left now—the words hung in the air between us.

Then a shadow severed the sunlight in the doorway, dispelling the moment. Two more visitors entered the workshop. Some potential customers perhaps. I smiled at Luis, thanking him. 'Buen trabajo,' my parting wish. Grasping my hand firmly, he shook it and in a clear voice said, 'Adios.' As I went out into the heat of the cobbled street once more, one of the goldfinches was preening its dusty feathers.

A Long Shot

It was George's idea. I was working when he visited so he wandered into the university library to browse the shelves until my return. On the bottom shelf of the botany section a book caught his eye. Flora Malesiana had a single due date stamp on the first page showing that it had been checked out once, twenty five years previously. It looked sad and old, with crinkled pages and fading colour plates. In it, George found a reference to balanaphoraceae, a tropical plant family with just forty or so species worldwide and, recorded in a few isolated locations in Indonesia.

I was unimpressed, and sensed trouble ahead. 'Balana what?' I asked with a frown. 'How are we supposed to find something that rare growing up a mountain in South East Asia?'

My objection was squashed and a few months later 'finding that plant' became the primary motive for our trip to Indonesia. We researched and planned in the manner that we thought we should for a botanical expedition but it was the pre-internet era so our resources were limited. They amounted to a return visit to the university library to delve more deeply into Flora Malesiana and a re-reading of our 'off the beaten track' guidebook for practical information about how to get there. This would have to do until we arrived in Indonesia.

Some months later in hot and humid Jakarta, the Tourist Information Office proved to be impressively uninformative about balanophoraceae. The two assistants conferred at length in Indonesian before letting us know that they didn't understand what we were talking about. Instead they tried to interest us in a side trip to Bali for 'very nice beach and very good temple.' I was tempted but George was not to be persuaded. We listened, declined politely, and left.

Undeterred we set out for Bogor in western Java to try our luck at Kebun Raya, the country's most prestigious botanic garden. We were slightly encouraged by the sign at its entrance, boasting of its 'serene and long-standing' status. In a dusty office, the man on duty was sleeping serenely, but luckily he was also head of special collections. We woke him and prepared to interrogate.

As it turned out, we probably knew more than he did about balanaphoraceae thanks to the invaluable Flora Malesiana. From the illustration we had seen that its appearance could hardly be described as attractive. The text described its colour as typically yellowish brown since it was lacking in chlorophyll; parasitic and with a fungal look about it. It grew to only a few inches in height and had a club-shaped bulb at its head. This was the inflorescence. Its similarity to a stubby phallus was most likely responsible for its sometime reputation as an aphrodisiac.

After some initial confusion over our hand-drawn picture, carefully copied from the book, the special collections man finally grasped what we were looking for and was able to confirm that balanophoraceae had, indeed, been found growing on the forested slopes of Gunung Gede, a volcanic mountain to the west of Bogor. He hadn't seen the plant himself although, fortunately, he knew what it looked like. He could offer no more information.

The next day, squeezed with fourteen other passengers into the back of a ten seater bemo, we journeyed on to Cibodas, one of the entry points for hiking up Mount Gede. From there our guidebook said, it would be possible to reach the summit in around ten hours with an overnight break at a shelter, purported to be somewhere on the way. After registering our intention at the small basecamp office—'just to climb the volcano,' we said in order to keep things simple—we set off along the cobbled path leading up into the forest. There at the start, it looked like the entry point to a neat, prize-winning village garden. I almost expected to see the trees all bearing Latin labels. They weren't; nevertheless my confidence increased a little. It might be a long shot but our plant might just be there, waiting for us. Maybe arrows would even point the way?

There were no arrows; only lush vegetation lined the way. And less than a hundred metres in, the best-kept garden-look totally disappeared. Leaves the size of dinner plates were competing to replace those recently hacked back and fronds of giant fern hung heavily across the path threatening to overrun it at any moment. The hungry insect life, which seemed to be emerging from a seven day fast, welcomed us into the rainforest. Towering over us, densely packed trees shielded the sunlight as we stepped deeper inside.

At first, we made frequent forays off the track, scanning around the base of the trees for something resembling that strange little plant that had inspired us. We had little idea of where to look and found nothing resembling our drawing. The muggy air and constant swatting of insects made walking hard work but every couple of hours we reached a resting point where the insects took the opportunity of another snack. Often there was a nearby stream from which to refill our water bottles. Rushing ever downwards, their velocity and noise increased, the higher we climbed.

More side forays followed, but no balanaphoraceae. Where would they grow? Were they even here? The trees wore mossy leggings now and reached out above ground with their twist-ed roots to trip the unwary. And the cobblestone path had all but disappeared giving way to hard baked soil. We needed to scramble over decaying tree trunks and bend double to pass under others that had fallen across the path. All were encased in a green carpet, wet velvet to the touch; criss-crossed with sprouting rows of orange toadstools. When we reached out for support, our hands sunk deep into their rotting flanks. As we climbed, we continued our search but with less and less con-viction.

Ahead of us, a waterfall announced itself and later a stream of volcanic hot water that gushed out noisily from a rock face, sending clouds of steam billowing out into the forest. The whole mountain was saturated in water.

Eventually we reached a tumbledown night shelter. It wasn't inviting. Inside many of the floorboards had rotted away but its corroded metal roof was still intact and would protect us from any rain. We unrolled our sleeping bags quietly. We were exhausted from climbing and disappointed not to have found our plant. Darkness fell suddenly and with it a veil of different forest sounds descended. We fell asleep to the relentless rasping of the night time cicadas.

But the night held a surprise. A scrabbling sound woke us around midnight. It came from the broken floorboards. Frantically, we flashed the torch across the room, expecting to see a large venomous snake swaying towards us. Instead, a pair of small, startled mammalian eyes stared back. A triangular head and spotted torso were poking up out of the floor. They belonged to a weasel-like creature. A palm civet, perhaps, out on a night forage. It surveyed us crossly then turned tail and left.

Morning came and with it, cooler air bringing a waft of realism. The scale of the challenge we had set ourselves dawned on us; we were ready to accept defeat gracefully. The final leg up to the summit didn't take long and we were rewarded with a stunning view over tropical forest from the volcano rim. There, growing at the top, we even found a plant we had not anticipated—a large clump of soft white stars—it was tropical edelweiss. Its felt-fashioned flowers were studded with tiny clinging pearls of dew. We were consoled. It was a good enough substitute for the elusive balanaphoraceae.

We began the long descent, intending to make it back to basecamp without stopping, then to hail a ride from a passing bemo back to Cibodas. But halfway down we did stop, on an impulse, to take a last peek into the jungly interior beside the path. And there, we found our plant waiting patiently for us. Half hidden by a large tree root, two unmistakeable brown fingers poked rudely up through the soil. A magic moment that caught us by surprise. I still have the photograph to prove it.

Senior Moments in Segovia

A high-speed RENFE train carries me calmly and efficiently into Segovia railway station. Around my sixtieth birthday an epiphany moment led first to retirement, and then brought me here. Like the younger backpacker, I am travelling to find myself—my sexagenarian self. It's also a Spanish speaking opportunity since I'm dutifully learning another language to keep my ageing grey matter alive.

West of Madrid, Segovia perches proud and Castilian; a rocky fortress on the Spanish plain. It's a compact city, and all roads lead conveniently into the expansive central plaza as if to ensure that I don't miss the city's most prized asset—a larger than life second century Roman aqueduct.

In fact, I can't miss it—it's a World Heritage colossus. Twenty-eight metres high and sixteen kilometres long, it pierces the square like an unfaltering vein of granite. 'Two tiers of 167 arches comprising 20,000 stones, built entirely without the use of mortar', my guidebook informs me. The sixty-year-old in me is unnerved and surreptitiously tests it with a push. Reassuringly, it stands firm so I sit down in a small plaza cafe beneath its arches to admire it some more, and rest my guidebook.

The camerero appears to take my order: 'Un café con leche y un pastel por favor.' Satisfied that he has understood, I flex my weary senior feet while the Segovian sun pampers my face. I enjoy the moment, owning my time. It's a retiree's prerogative.

Afterwards at the Aqueduct Interpretation Centre I can resume my learning before my guidebook wills me on to follow the water's subterranean route, helpfully signposted by twenty-four pavement plaques.

Later that day, with the mysteries of Roman water engineering fully clarified for me, I ponder where next. A medieval monastery, perhaps? Or the Alcazar? Maybe mañana. After all, for a senior who is in no hurry, there is always tomorrow.

Lightning Source UK Ltd.
Milton Keynes UK
UKHW041316080321
379983UK00002B/280